BALD EAGLES

Studies For Wildlife Artists

Photography and Text

by

Al Lodwick

First Edition 2015

ISBN 978-1514777602

DEDICATION

To Ann Lodwick, my wife and best friend nor nearly thirty-eight years.

ACKNOWLEDGEMENTS

Scott Mies for encouragement and editorial advice.

Rachel Lodwick for the Mieswick, LLC logo.

Victoria Tubbs for the author's photograph.

INTRODUCTION

This book is the result of five years of nature photography in the biologically diverse central highlands of Arizona around Prescott. The Arizona highlands are not what most people imagine when they think of Arizona. At the lowest level you find desert grassland. This gives way to Oak-Pinyon-Juniper woodland. Higher still are the tall Ponderosa Pines – a stand of trees stretching hundreds of miles in Arizona and New Mexico. At the highest levels you find Douglas Fir forest. Throughout the highlands you find an intermingling of both flora and fauna from both hotter and colder climates. For example, you can find hedgehog cacti growing at the roots of Ponderosa Pines.

Perching in the Ponderosa Pines, particularly those that have died, but are still standing, you may find the majestic symbol of the United States, the Bald Eagle. They have become accustomed to seeing people and will allow you to approach fairly close on many occasions.

The emphasis of this book is to depict scenes for wildlife artists that are not easily seen with the unaided eye. Examples of this are the positions of the eyes, how the talons grasp branches and the design of individual feathers and how they overlap.

The author hopes that non-artists will also enjoy the pictures and learn more about these powerful birds and the habitats of the highlands of central Arizona.

Al Lodwick
Prescott, Arizona
June 2015

PERCHING

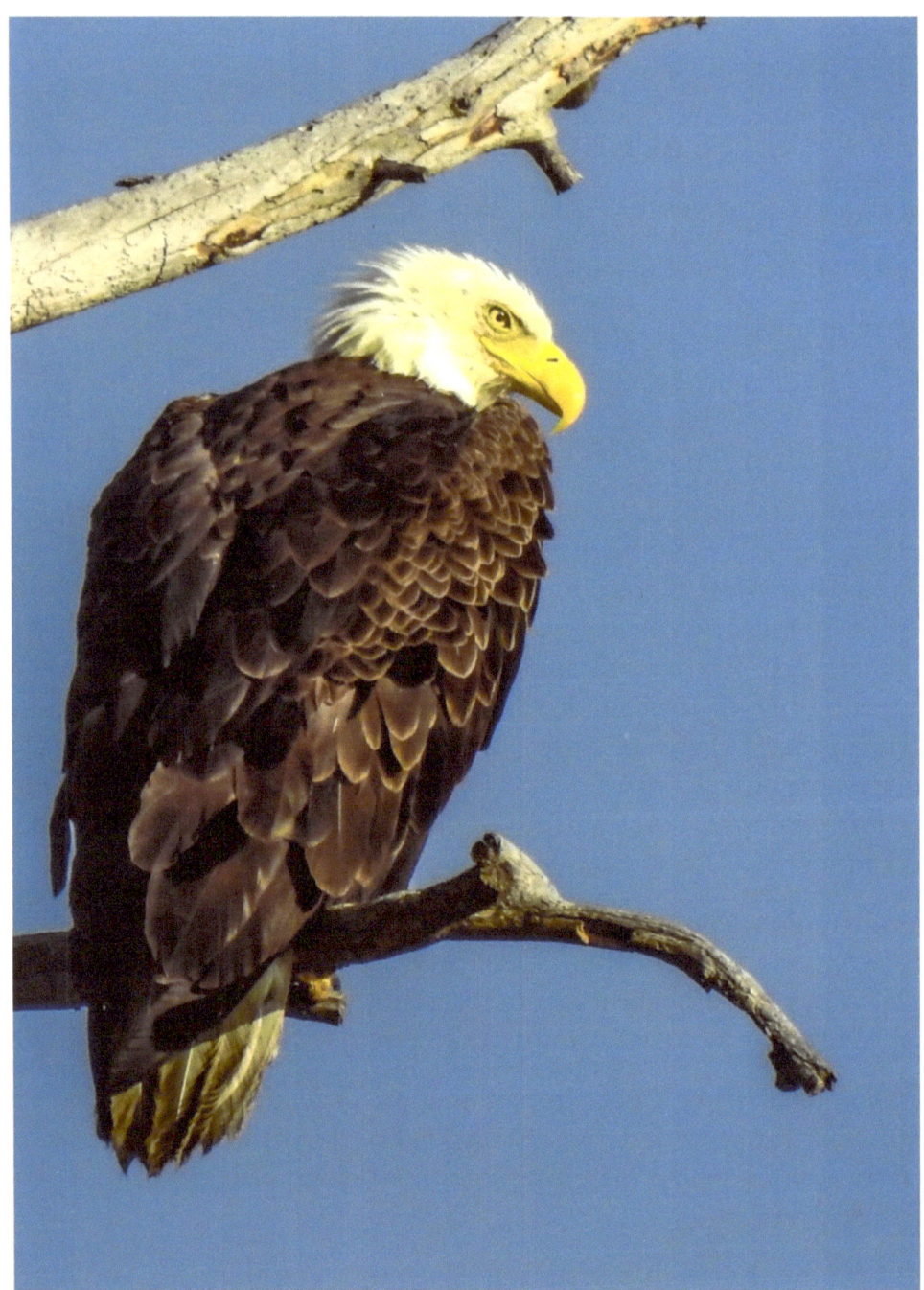

A Bald Eagle's eyes quickly draw your attention. Some references say that these birds can spot a rabbit up to two miles from their perch. They also are able to spot a mouse on the ground when flying at 650 feet above it.

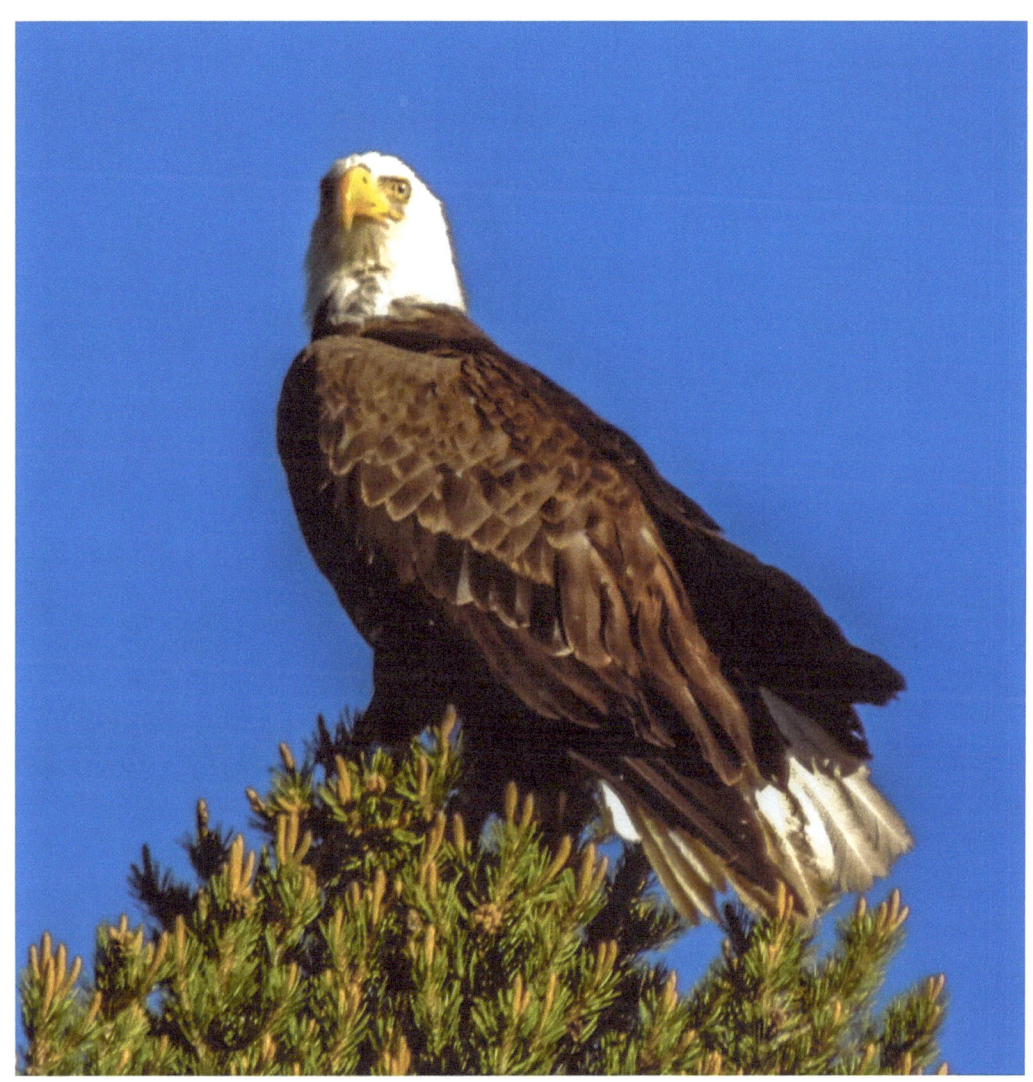

This Bald Eagle picture shows two unusual things. First, it is perched in a live tree. Usually they perch in dead trees. Second, it is in a Pinyon Pine tree. Usually they choose Ponderosa Pines for their perches. You can distinguish between the two by the length of the needles – Ponderosa needles are much longer than these.

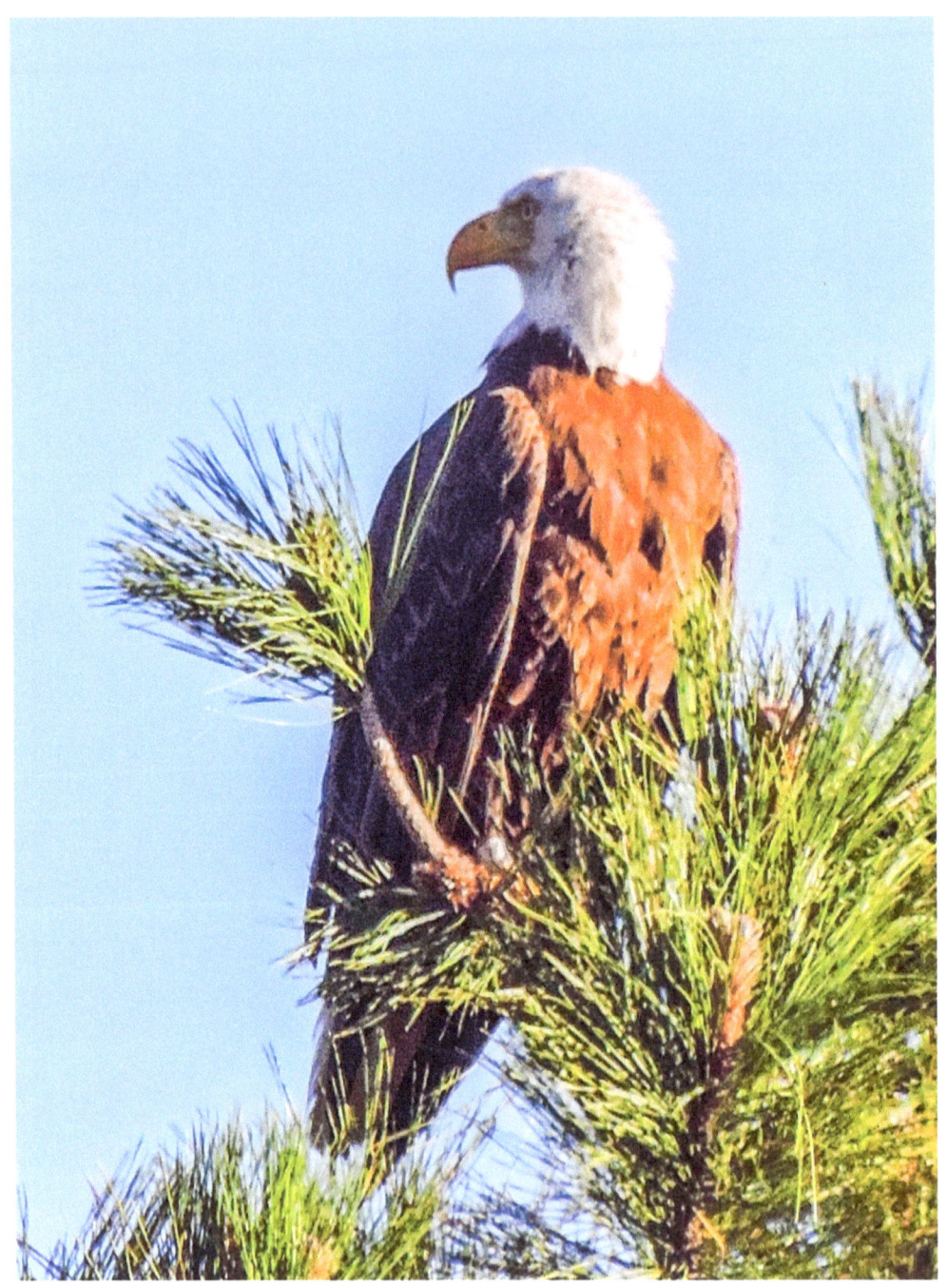

This Bald Eagle is perched in a live Ponderosa Pine tree. Compare the length of the needles on the Pinyon Pine in the previous picture to distinguish between the two species. Having both types of trees is typical of the transition zone of the central Arizona highlands.

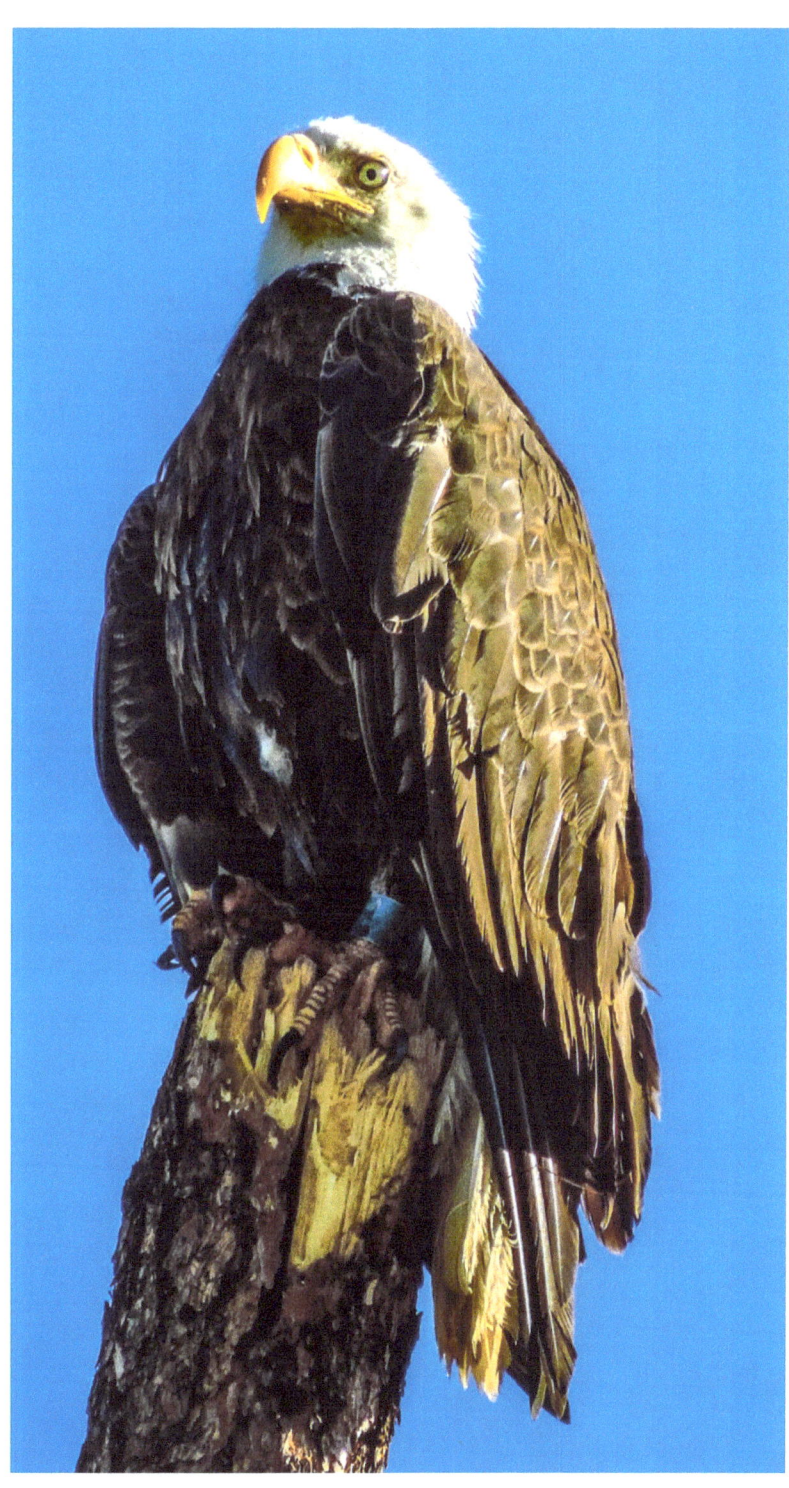

This picture illustrates both the toes and the talons of a Bald Eagle. Toes and talons are often used interchangeably but they are two different things like toes and toenails.

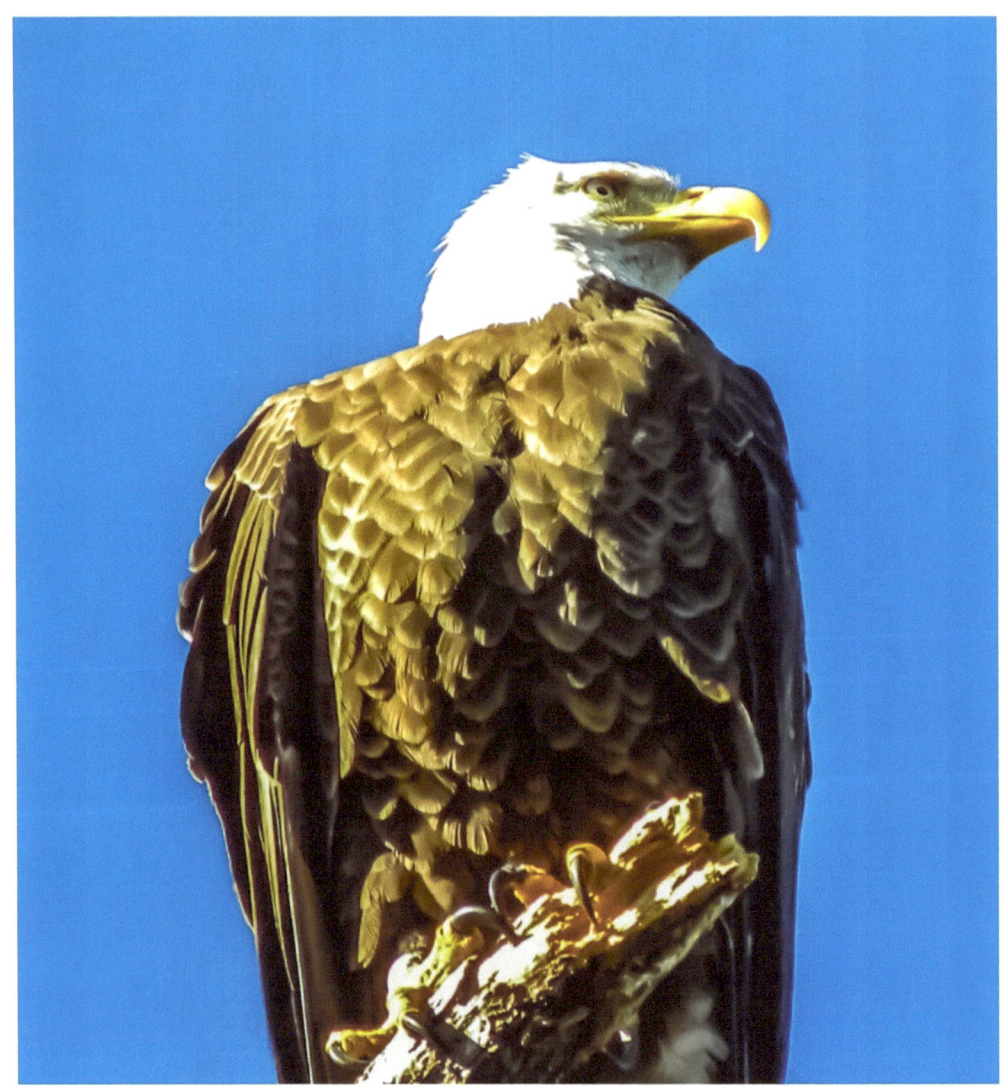

The foot of a Bald Eagle is about 6 inches long. This is unusually large for any bird, including raptors. A strong human can exert a grip pressure of about 40 pounds per square inch. An adult Bald Eagle can exert a grip pressure of about 400 pounds per square inch. When you couple this with the sharp talons it is obvious that its prey undergoes a quick death.

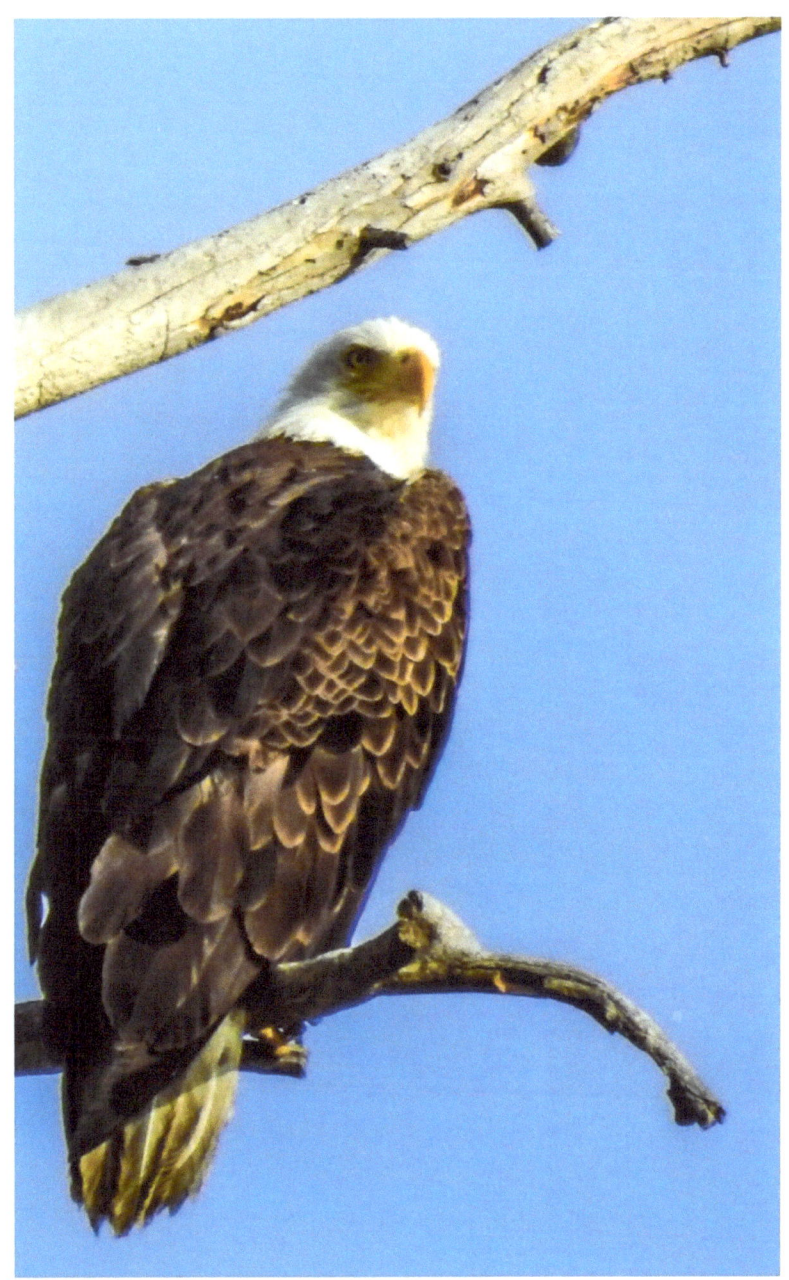

This picture shows the shadow of the Bald Eagle's bill across its face in the late afternoon sun

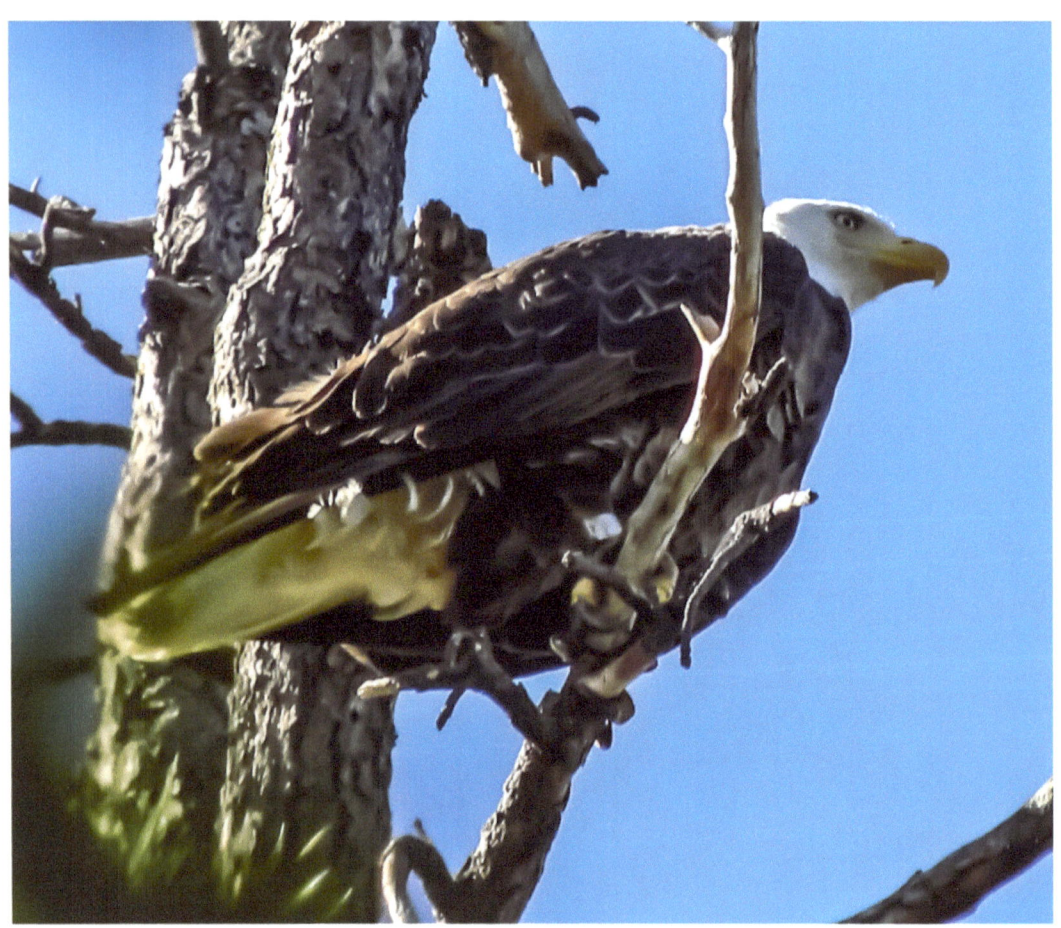

The intense gaze and nervously flicking tail indicate that this Bald Eagle is about to fly from its perch in pursuit of a fish. You can also see the leg band that is applied to most Bald Eagles before they fledge.

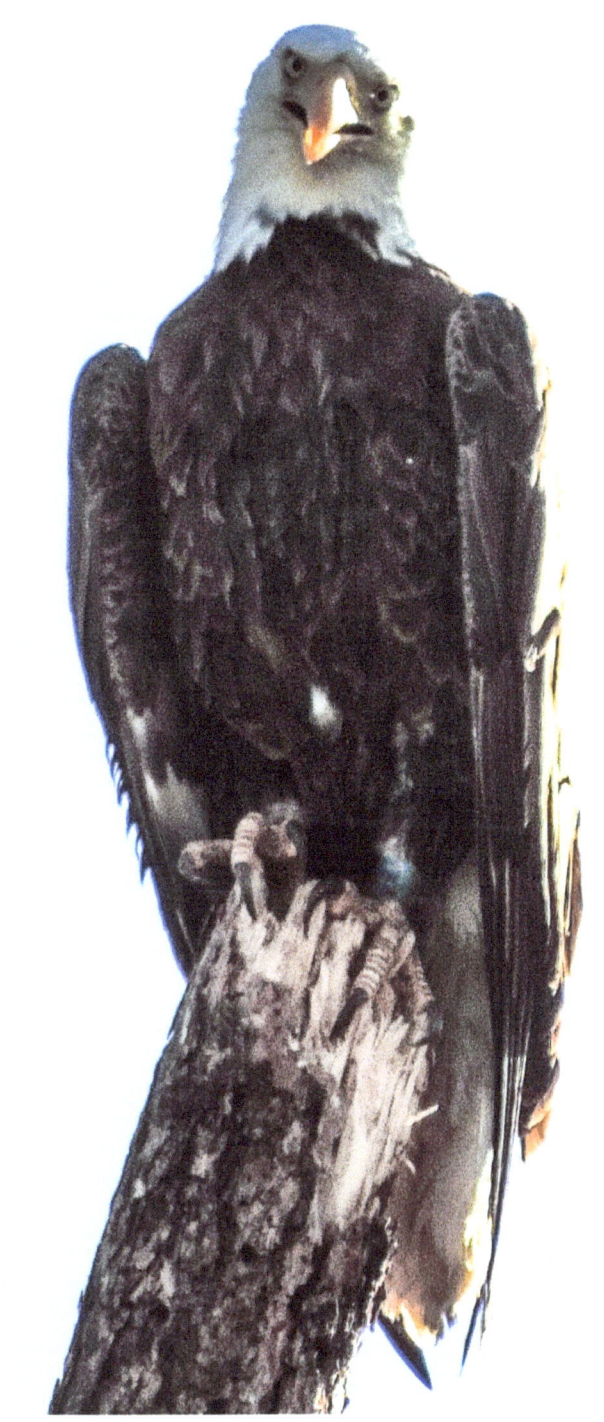

Bald Eagles develop characteristics similar to humans and other animals. This bird seems to enjoy sitting with its head cocked to its left.

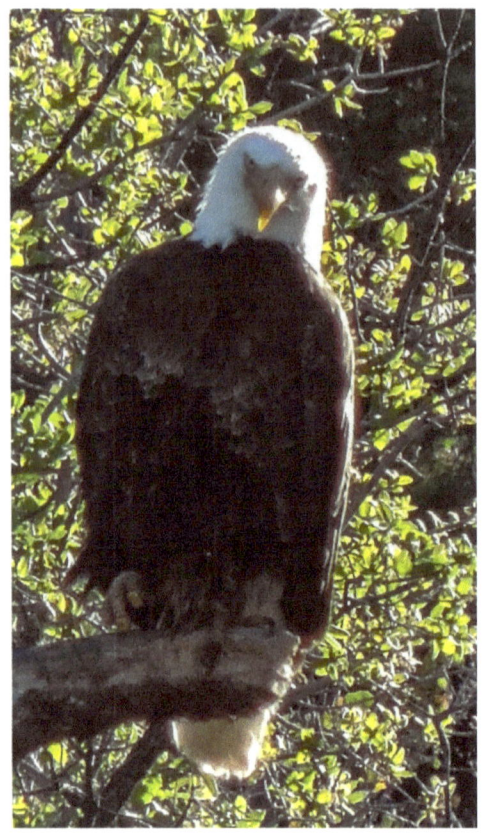 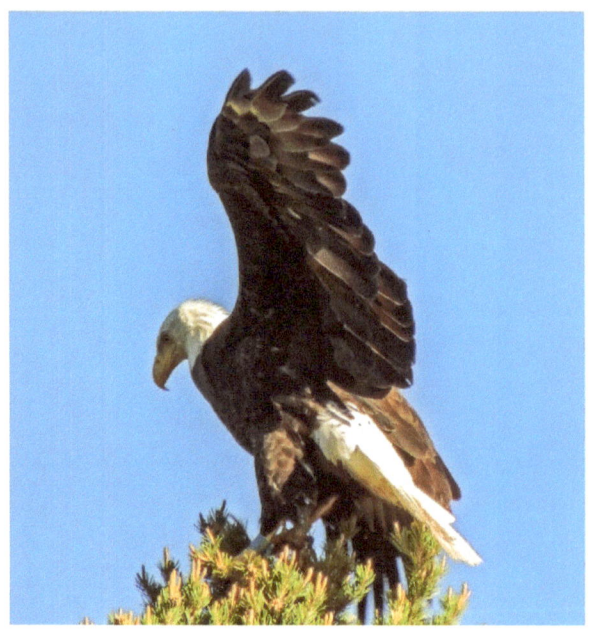

Bald Eagles are the second-largest birds in North America. Only the California Condor is larger. However, they are not actually bald. The white feathers on their head lead to the name "bald". The white feathers do not usually appear until they are three to five years of age. The greater the percentage of white the closer they are to full maturity. Some birds reach maturity after three years of age just as humans mature at different ages.

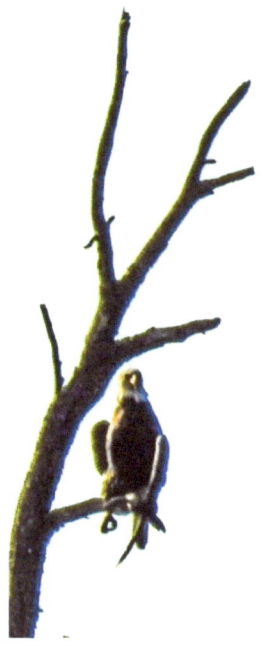 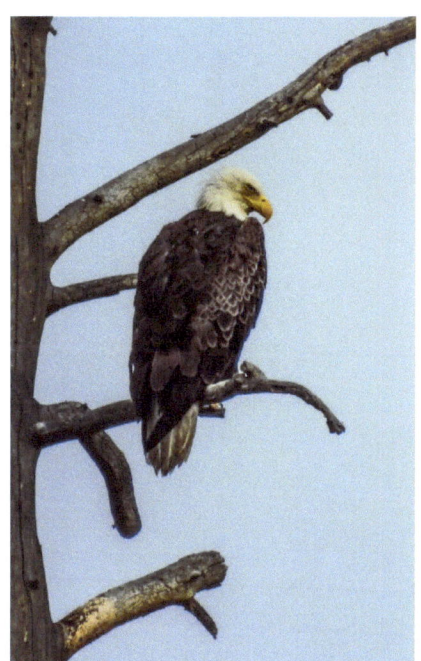

Bald Eagles do not typically perch on one leg the way that many other birds do. In the left picture the bird is holding its foot in an unusual position – perhaps it has been injured.

Bald Eagles have what is called a nicitating membrane. This functions as a third eyelid. It sweeps across the eye every few seconds to wipe away specks of dirt and to moisten the eye. It is somewhat translucent but the Bald Eagle still has excellent vision when it is covering the eye. If it actually had to blink its eyelid closed as often as humans do, it would lose some of its competitive advantage as a predator.

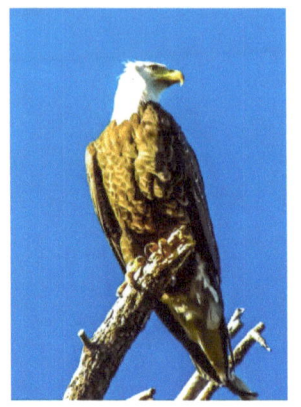

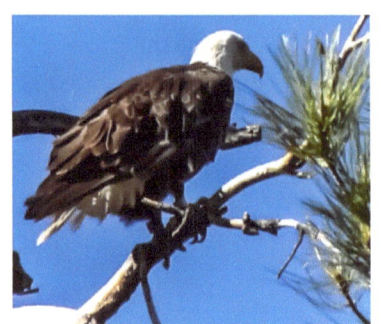

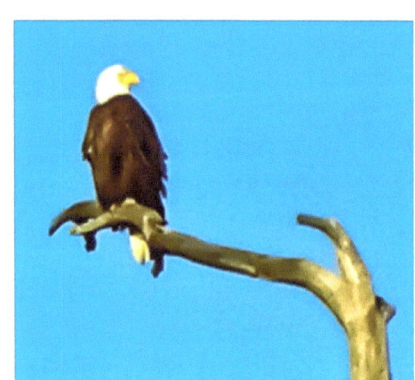

While the Bald Eagle is the symbol of The United States, during the 1960s and 1970s it was nearly wiped out. The use of pesticides such as DDT had gotten into the food chain and was ingested by the birds. This caused a metabolic change that led to eggs having very thin shells. The shells then cracked while they were being incubated. As a result few birds were born. Once the use of DDT was banned the birds began to recover and are no longer threatened or endangered.

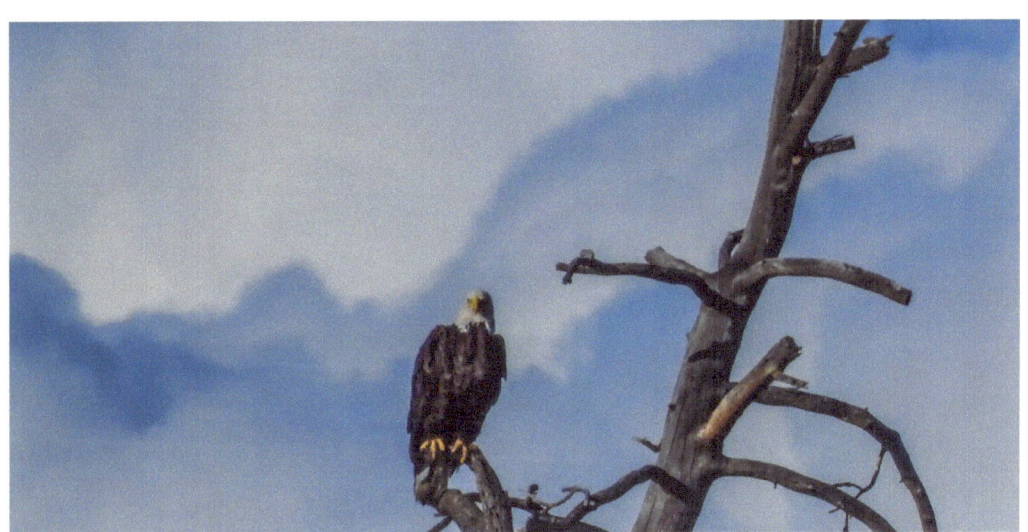

Female Bald Eagles are about 25% larger than males. Their body is about 3 feet long with a wingspan of about 7 feet. A male's body averages about 4 inches shorter and his wingspan is between 6 and 7 feet. They weigh about 10 to 14 pounds. The farther north they live, the bigger they tend to be.

PAIRS

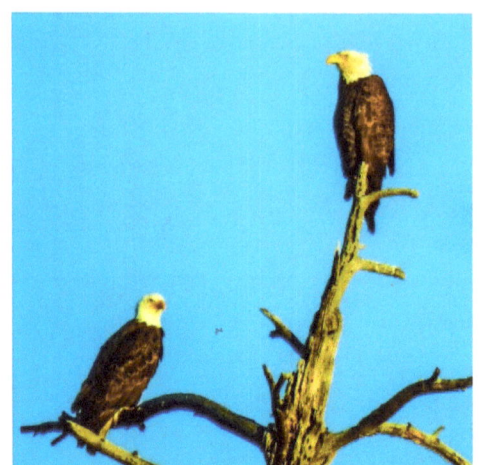

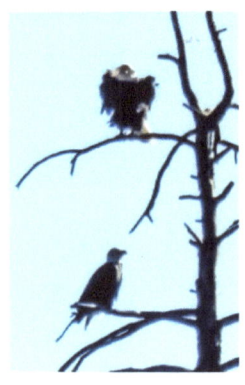

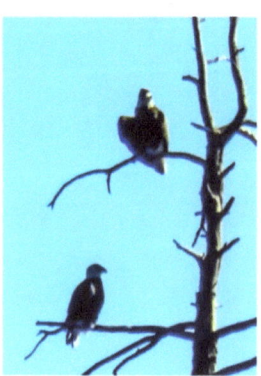

It is nearly impossible to tell the male from the female because the way that they fluff their feathers and hold their wings out from their bodies makes it hard to compare sizes.

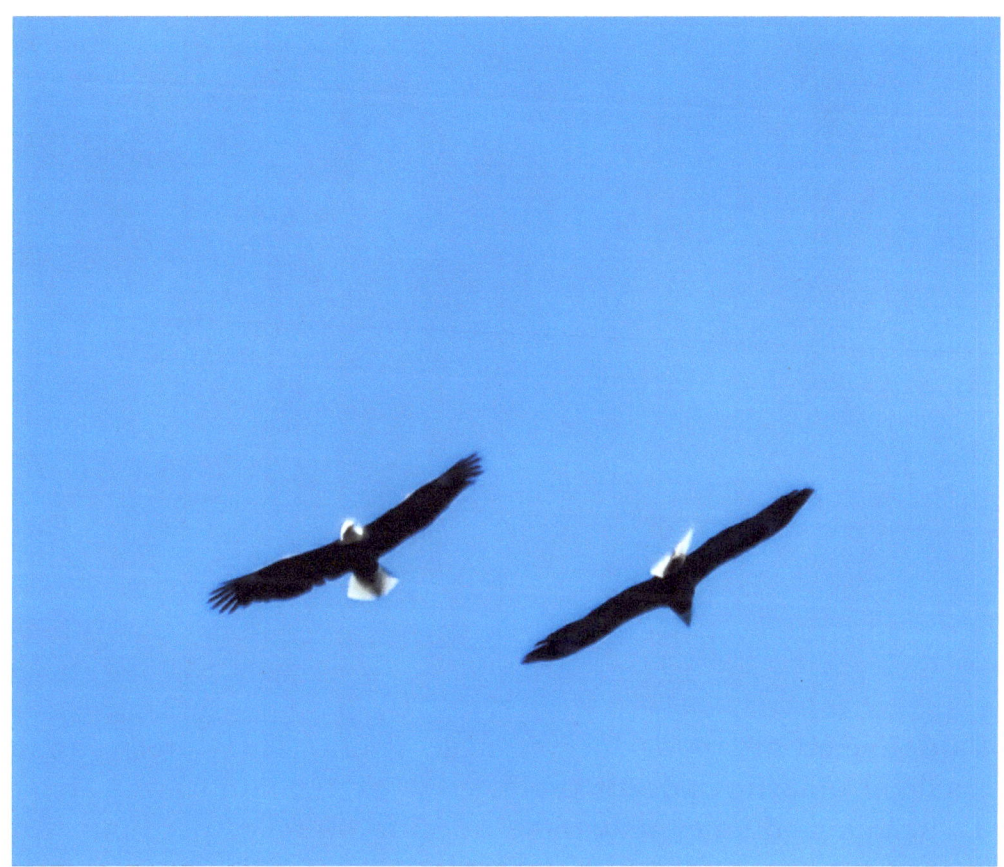

Although Bald Eagles stay with the same mate for life they will still go through the mating ritual. In the fall they will fly around each other as if they are at a dance. Sometimes they lock talons and tumble through the air. However, this is not mating. Mating occurs when they are perched.

FLIGHT

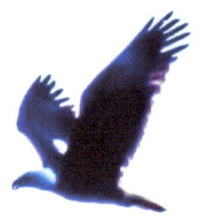

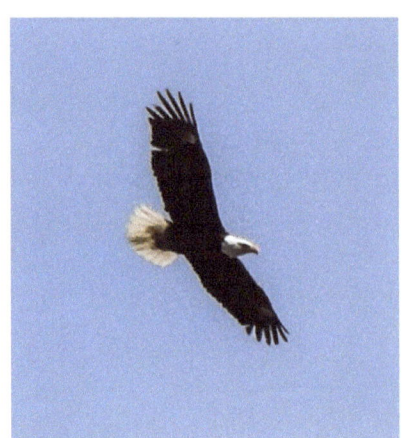

   Bald Eagles are powerful yet agile flyers. They prefer an almost effortless flight utilizing updrafts produced when the sun warms area on the ground. In this mode they may move at 35 to 40 miles per hour while not expending much energy flapping their wings. When diving on prey it can reach 75 to 100 miles per hour.

   Imagine being hit with something weighing 10 pounds moving at 100 miles per hour and that grabs you with sharp talons that squeeze with 10 times more force than a human.

JUVENILES

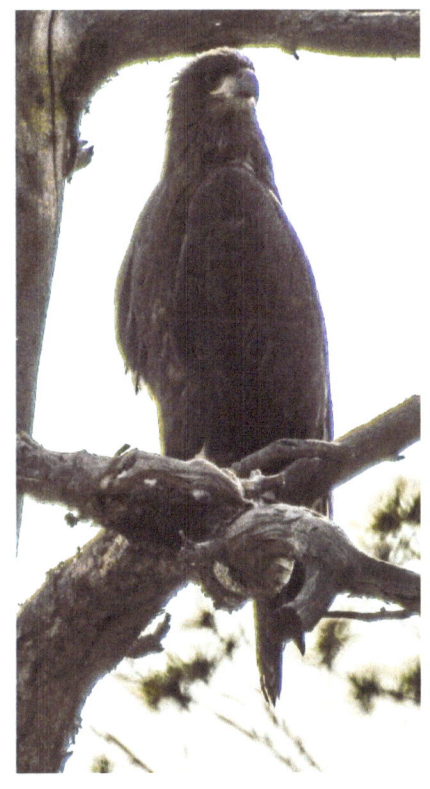 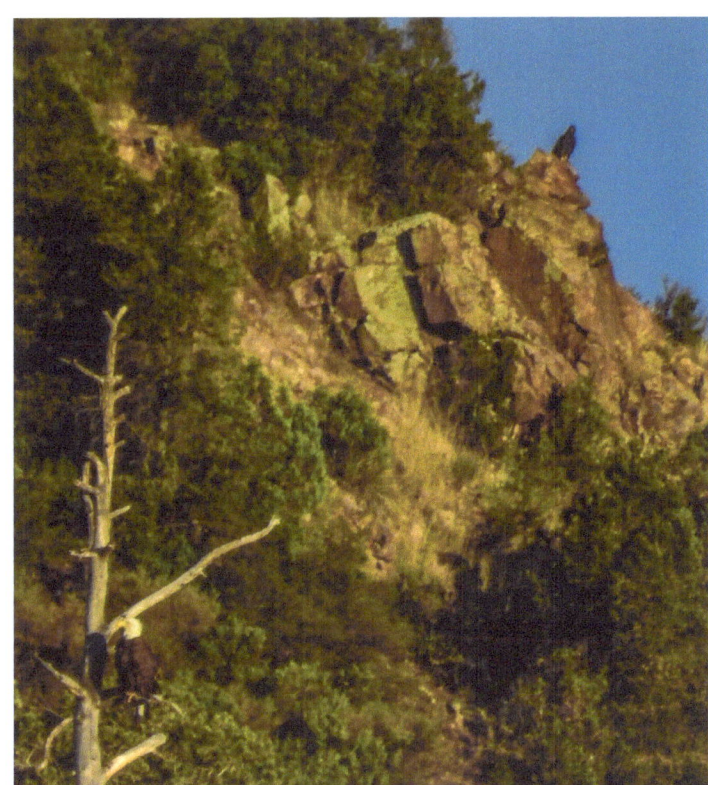

The author is certain that the bird in the left picture is the same one as in the upper-right corner of the other picture. The reason for this is that the close-up was taken only a few days after the other picture and just below the rock face in that picture. Typically only one bird will live to fledge (fly from the nest) each year. The juvenile is nearly the same size as its parents at only about five months of age. As a juvenile grows it will develop white streaking that will persist until maturity when its body will become uniformly brown and it will have the characteristic white head.

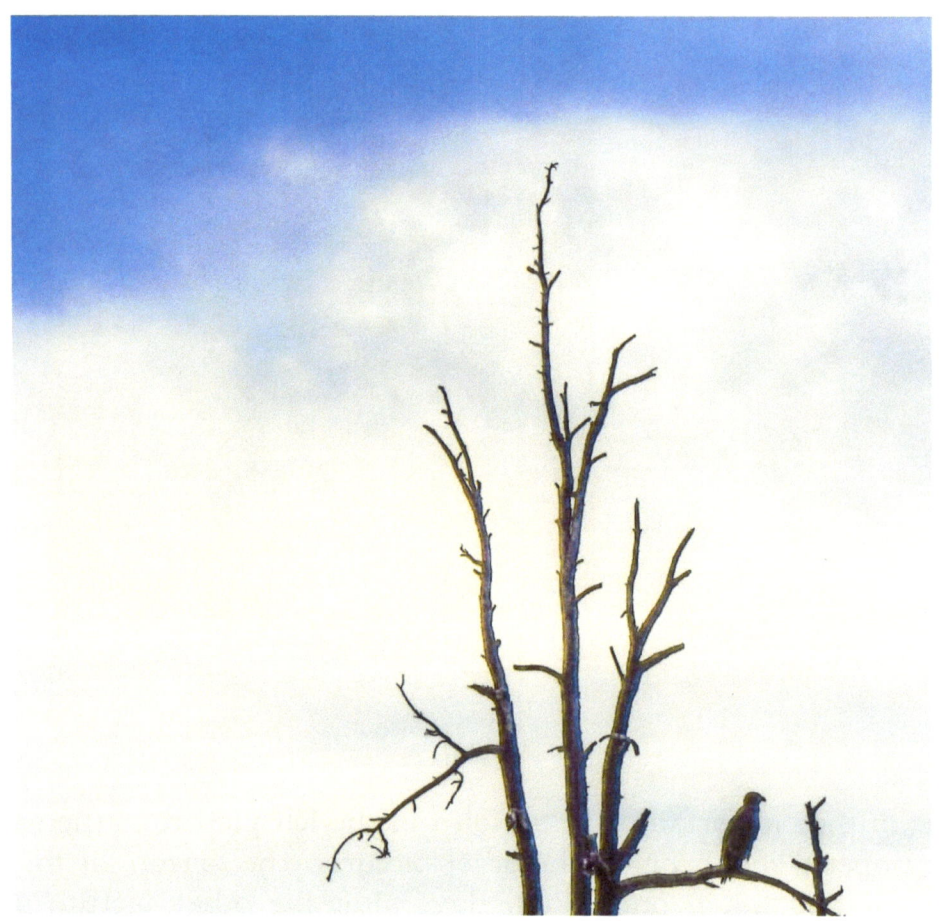

Solitude. That is what this picture says. The adult Bald Eagles have completed their mission for this cycle of life. The juvenile has been taught to fend for itself and the parents have left the area for the summer. The young bird is all alone in the world. It does not know what is in store for it. When the parents return in a few months they will drive the yearling away so that there will be sufficient food for the young that they will raise next year.

INTERACTIONS WITH OTHER BIRDS

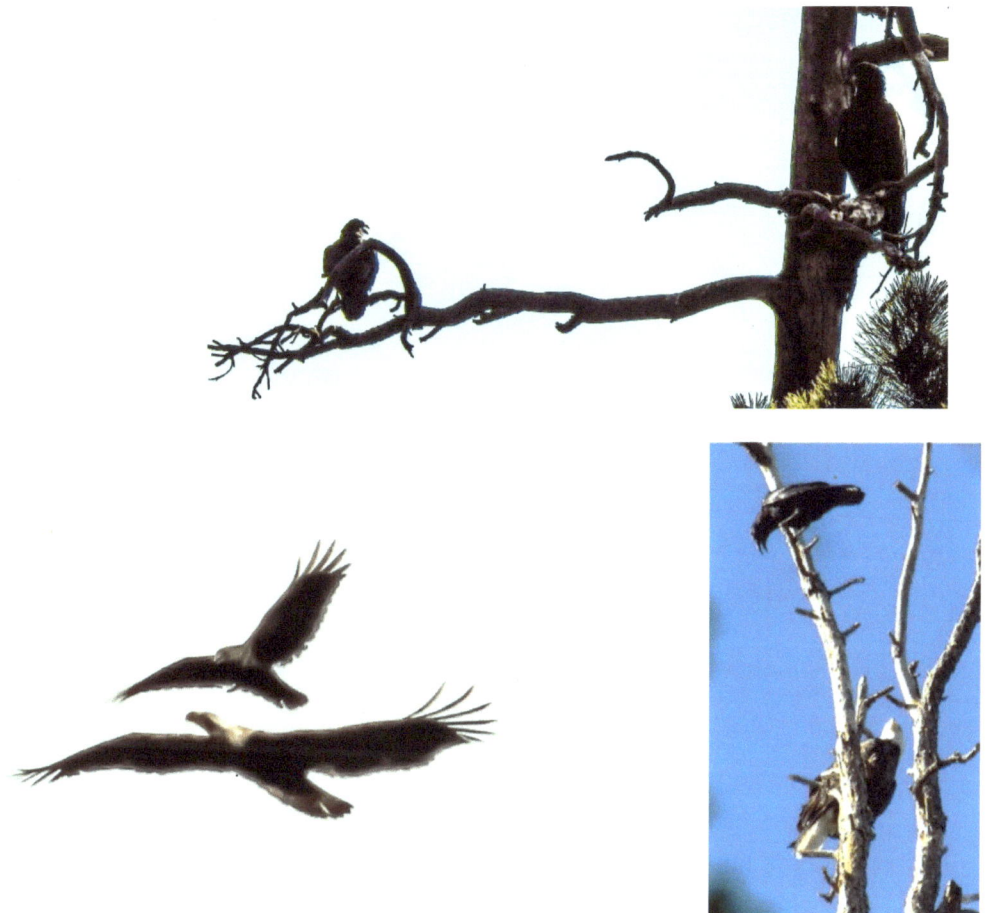

It is obvious from these pictures that the Common Raven gives up a lot in size when it goes against a Bald Eagle. However, the raven has a large and powerful bill. While the author was taking pictures of the juvenile Bald Eagle a Common Raven landed only a few feet away and encouraged the eagle to move on. Even though it is young, the eagle seems to know that it has little to fear. It is a different story in the lower left picture. It seems likely that the Bald Eagle ventured too close to a Common Raven's nest and like most parents it will viciously defend its eggs or young. The lower right picture shows a fascinating scene. The Bald Eagle landed in a dead Ponderosa Pine already occupied by a Common Raven. Demonstrating its intelligence, the raven pulled chunks of dead wood off the tree and dropped them on the eagle. Not only did the raven use a tool, it used a weapon! It seemed to work because the eagle flew to a new tree a short distance away.

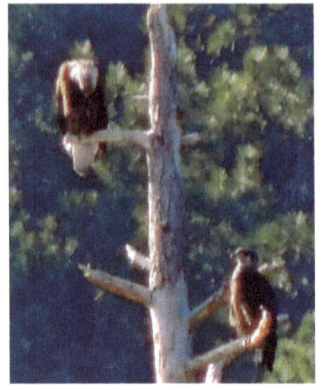 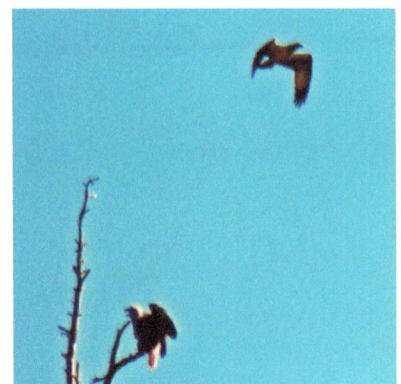

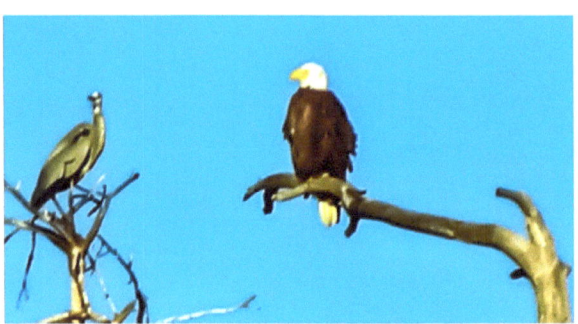

The top two pictures show interactions between a Bald Eagle and an Osprey. The Osprey depends almost exclusively on fish for food. Bald Eagles will catch other prey but they prefer fish for their diet, diving on a fish that is near the top of the water. Therefore, whenever they meet there is conflict. This is especially true when the eagles are about to nest or have an active nest. The osprey is slightly smaller than the eagle but otherwise they are pretty evenly matched. The battles can rage for hours. The eagle almost always wins but even as the osprey is retiring from the battlefield it will sometimes take one final swipe at the eagle's head with its talons. If a Bald Eagle sees an Osprey catch a fish it will attack the Osprey and almost always cause it to drop the fish.

Great Blue Herons and Bald Eagles also share a preference for fish but they are more tolerant of each other. This is probably because the heron catches fish by wading near the shore while the eagle dives on fish further out in the water. When this heron chose a spot very close to where an eagle was already perched the eagle screamed very loudly and non-stop until the other bird moved away.

CLOSE-UPS FOR GETTING THE DETAILS JUST RIGHT

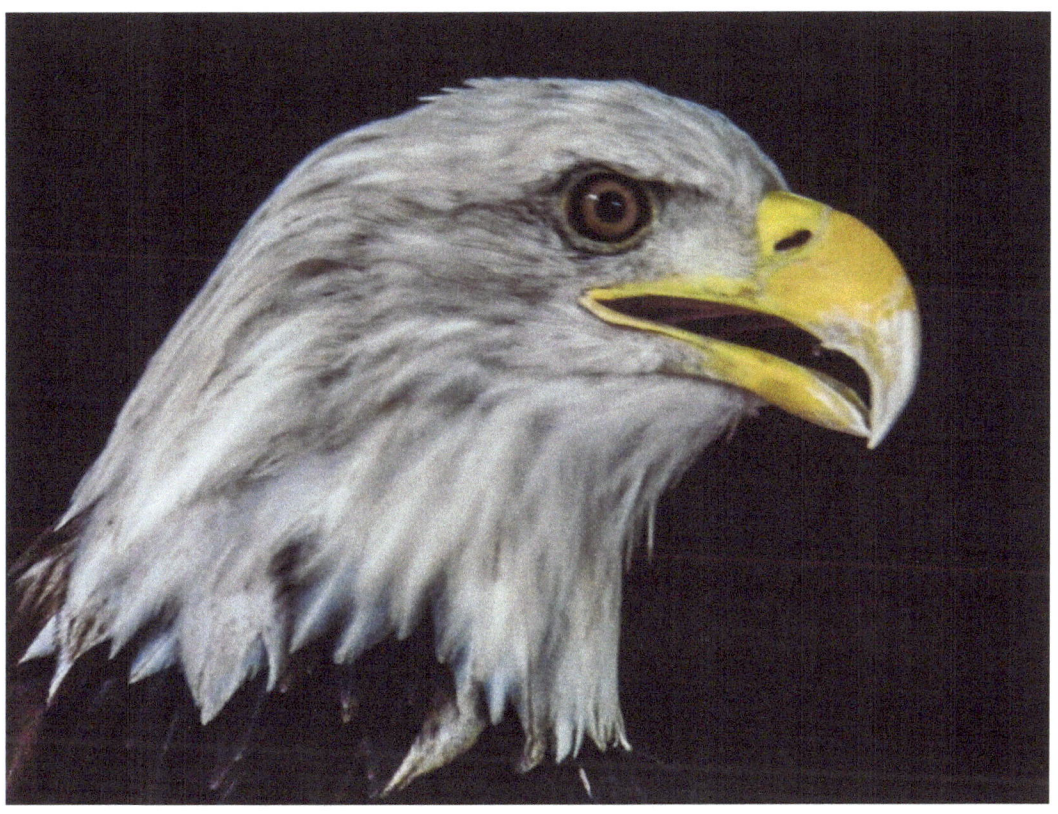

This is the head of a Bald Eagle that is probably about three years old. The white feathers are developing but there are still streaks of brown at this age. Also, the bill has not yet turned fully yellow. In about another year or two these changes will be complete and it will be mature for breeding. Compare this to the head of the mature bird on the next page.

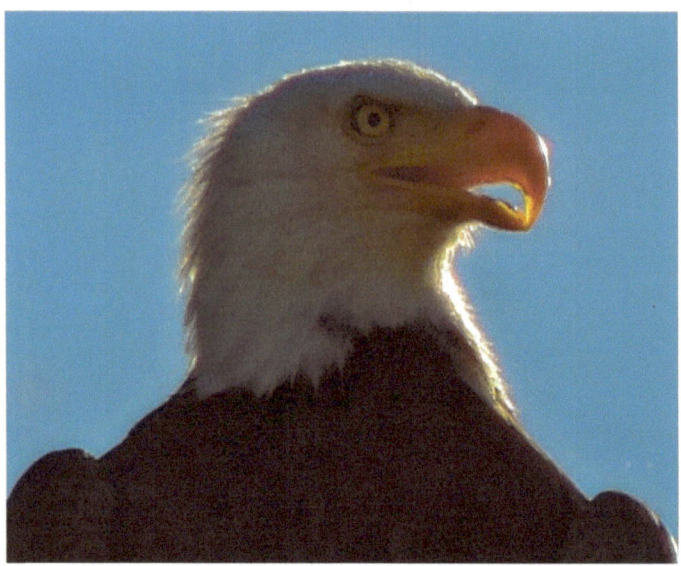

By comparing this picture with the one on the previous page you can see the changes that occur over about a two year period while the bird is maturing.

You can also understand why bird identification is an art as well as a science. If you had only the previous picture and compared it to popular field guides you might not decide that it is a Bald Eagle because it does not exactly match the picture of a juvenile nor an adult.

Also note the shape of the shoulders in this picture. The upright posture and hunched shoulders are good indications that you are looking at a Bald Eagle.

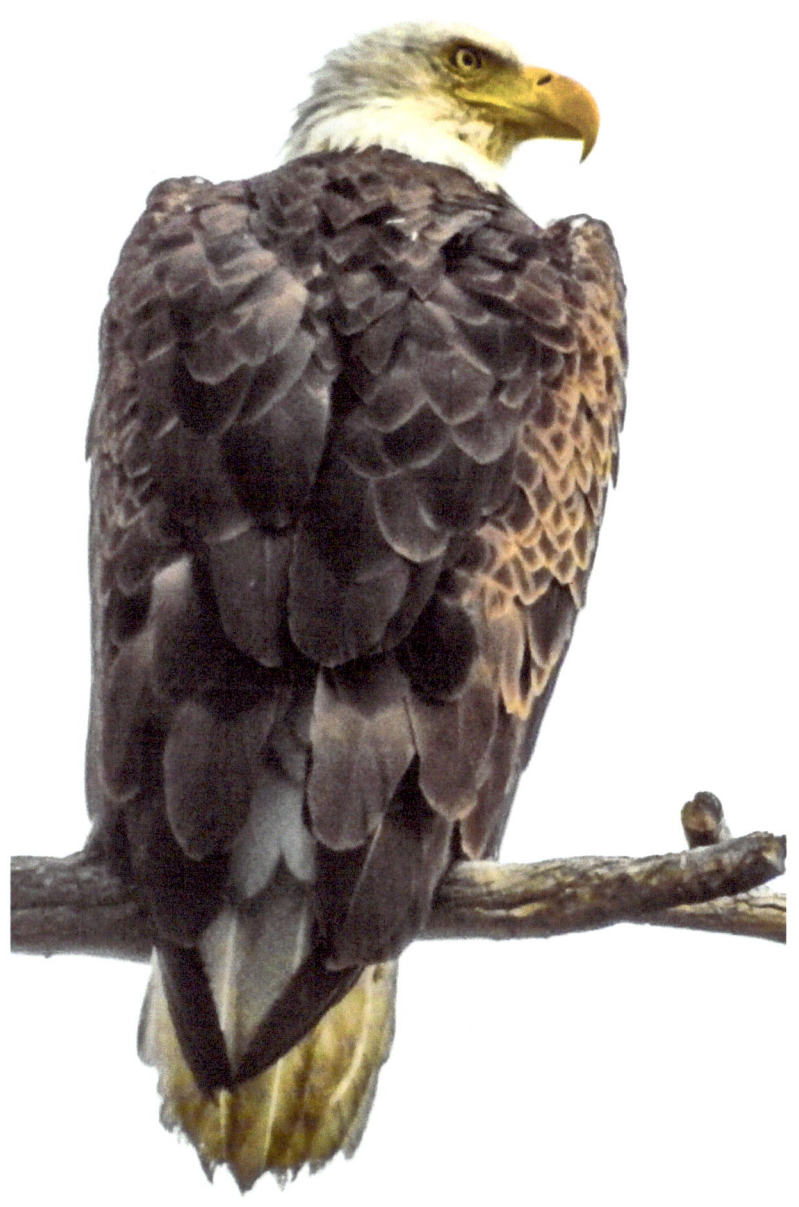

      Notice how the feathers from the tips of the wings meet at a point over the tail. It is also rare to see a Bald Eagle's legs since they are covered with feathers.

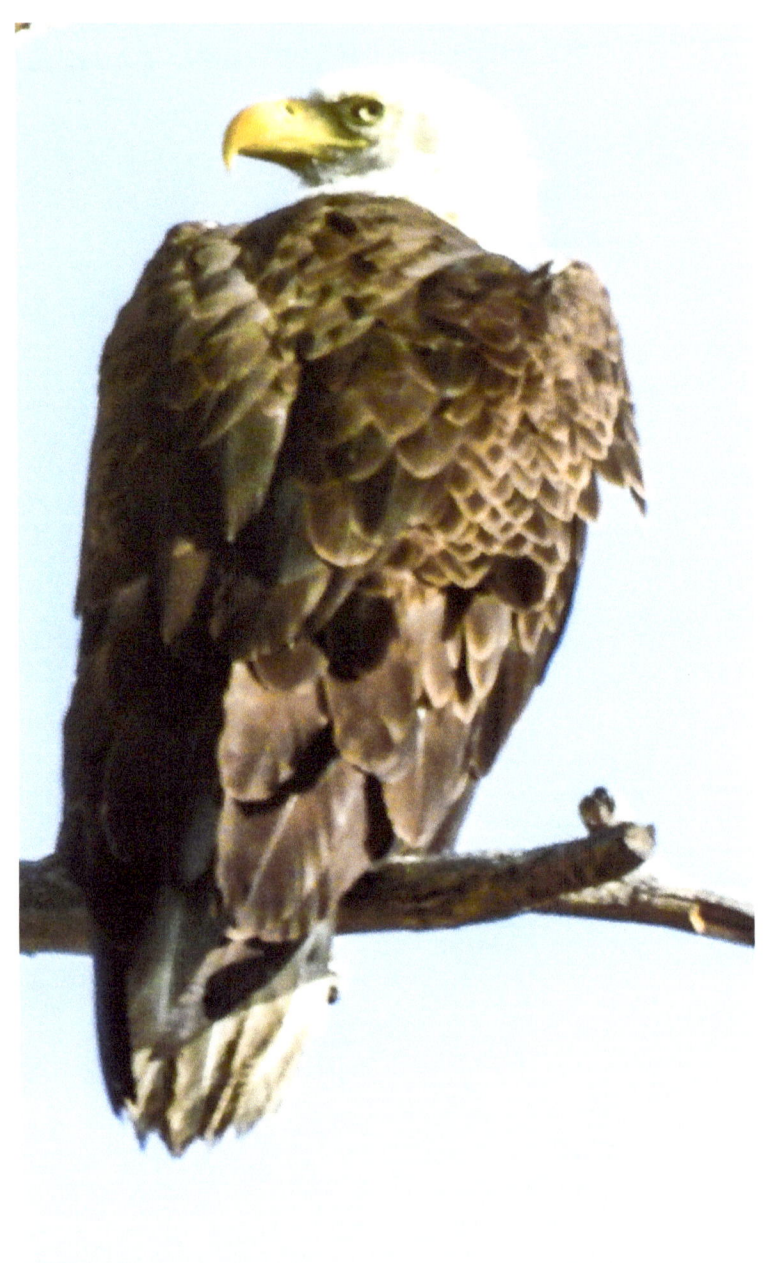

This picture is not sharply focused but it is included because it illustrates the importance of the eye in Bald Eagle pictures. Since the bill is not flexible, the eye defines the expression on its face. Compare this menacing looking eye with the more majestic eye in the previous photo.

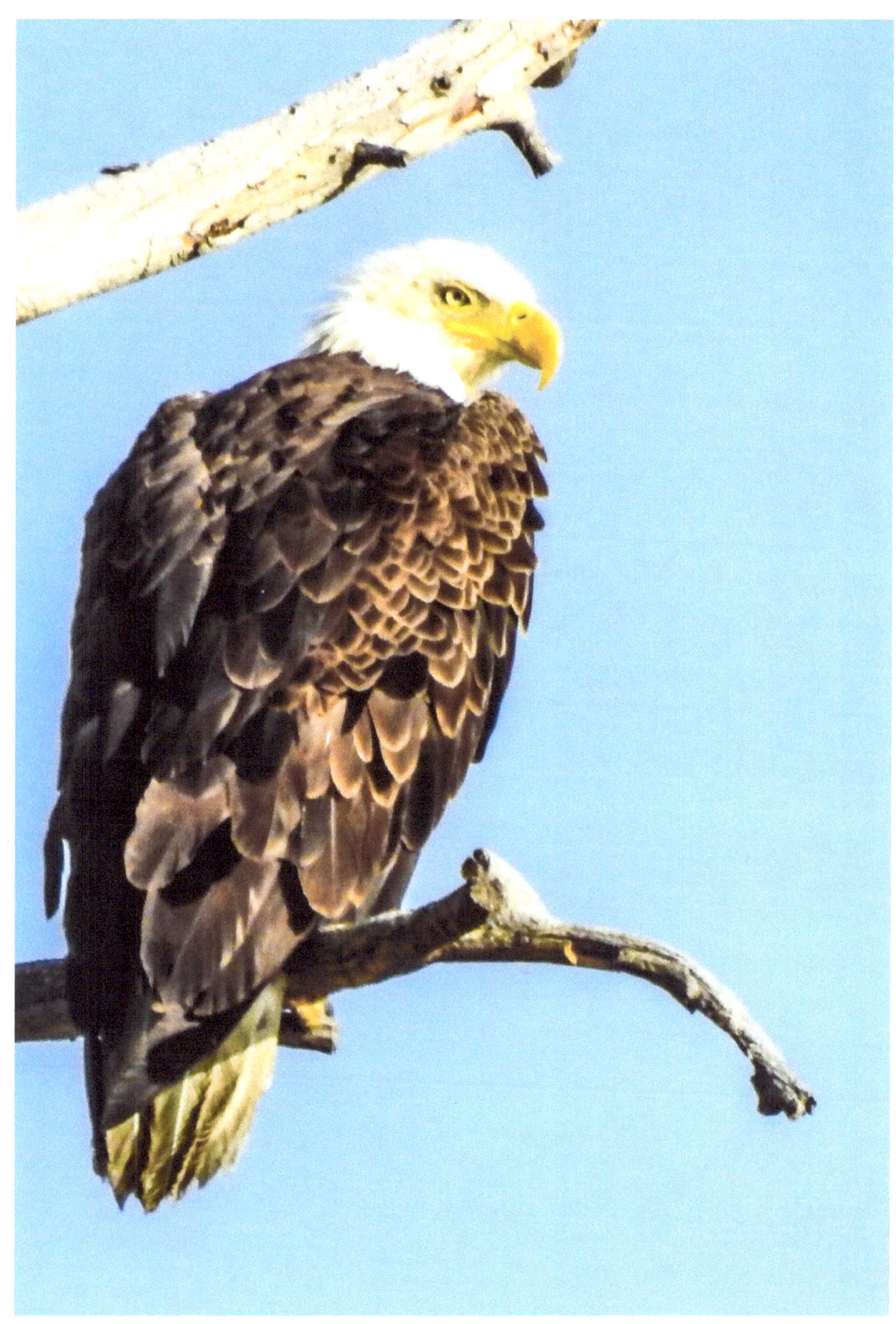

Again, compare the eye in this picture with the ones in the previous pictures. Here the eyelid is very slightly closed and there is also some shadow on the eye giving the bird the appearance of being tired.